Hamid Sulaiman

FREEDOM HOSPITAL

Translated by Francesca Barrie

Interlink Books

An imprint of Interlink Publishing Group, Inc.
Northampton, Massachusetts

First American edition published in 2018 by

INTERLINK BOOKS
An imprint of Interlink Publishing Group, Inc.
46 Crosby Street, Northampton, Massachusetts 01060
www.interlinkbooks.com

Library of Congress Cataloging-in-Publication Data available
ISBN 978-1-62371-995-1 • paperback
ISBN 978-1-62371-994-4 • hardback

Printed and bound in the United States of America

ROYAUME-UNI

This book is supported by the Institut français (Royaume-Uni) as part of the Burgess programme

Supported using public funding by

**ARTS COUNCIL
ENGLAND**

This book has been selected to receive financial assistance from English PEN's "PEN Translates" programme, supported by Arts
Council England. English PEN exists to promote literature and our understanding of it, to uphold writers' freedoms around the
world, to campaign against the persecution and imprisonment of writers for stating their views, and to promote the friendly
co-operation of writers and the free exchange of ideas. www.englishpen.org

Culture Resource

The author received a grant to create this book from the Culture Resource (Al Mawred Al Thaqafi)

With thanks to Coline Houssias, Khalil Bendib, Nizar Toulaimat, Anne Clerc, Ammar Abd Rabbo, Aurélie Ruby,
Mariam Al-Awani, Pauline Amelin, Élodie Remy, Henriette Souk and to the publishers, Serge and Isabelle.

This book is dedicated to my friend Hussam Khayat (1989-2013) who walked beside me at the Damascus demonstrations, and who was tortured to death in prison by the Syrian secret police.

YASMIN
Born in Damascus in April 1984, Yasmin grew up in a moderate Sunni family. She lived with her family in the United Arab Emirates for ten years, before returning to study Pharmacy at Aleppo University, completing her Master's in Damascus. She is due to start a PhD in the U.S. Like many young people, Yasmin threw herself into the revolution. She runs an underground hospital, Freedom Hospital, in Houria, a town in northern Syria.

SOPHIE
Born in Damascus in 1980, Sophie and her family left Syria to live in France when she was eight years old and she became a journalist following her studies at Sciences Po in Paris. She and Yasmin were childhood friends; they spent their holidays together in Damascus. When the revolution breaks out, only journalists working for pro-Assad organisations are allowed to enter the country. Sophie decides to smuggle herself back in to make a documentary about Freedom Hospital and its occupants.

ABU TAYSIR
Born in Hama in 1953, Abu Taysir survived the massacres that took place in the city in 1982, but he witnessed the execution of his brother and cousins. Accused by the regime of being a member of the Muslim Brotherhood (when he was in fact a communist at the time), in total he has spent eleven years behind bars. He took part in the very early demonstrations and following the regime's massacre of tens of thousands of civilians, he joins forces with the Muslim Brotherhood, eventually taking charge of the local branch of the Free Syrian Army.

ABU AZAB
Born in Aleppo in 1982, Azab is working as a mechanic when the revolution begins. Initially pro-Bashar, he sees the revolution as a conspiracy against the wise rule of Assad, until his pregnant wife and two children are killed by Syrian army bombing. It is then that he joins the Free Syrian Army.

'ONE EYED' ELIAS/JAMAL
Born in 1981 in Qamishli, Elias is Assyrian and a practising Christian. He moves to Qatar for work at the beginning of the revolution. Shortly afterwards, he quits his job and returns to Syria to take part in demonstrations going on in his hometown. He is arrested during one of these demonstrations and tortured by the secret police, who suspect him of being sent by Prince Hamad of Qatar to bring down the regime. He loses an eye under torture in prison.

HAVAL
Born in 1988 in the Kurdish district of Zor Ava in Damascus, Haval has a Master's degree in Philosophy. He is doing his military service when the revolution breaks out and deserts his post when he is ordered to open fire on protesters. Wounded by army gunfire in the course of a demonstration, he is awaiting a kidney transplant. He is being treated at Freedom Hospital, but doesn't strictly need to be there every day – he stays to be near Zahabiah as much as possible.

DR YAZAN

Born in 1972 in Daraa, the birthplace of the revolution in Southern Syria in 2011, Yazan comes from a Sunni family and is close to the Muslim Brotherhood. He is married with two young daughters, having gained his medical degree in Damascus in 1996. At the beginning of the revolution, Yazan treats rebels in secret, which gets him thrown in prison. Having escaped from Damascus, he sends his family to a refugee camp in Turkey, and sets off for Northern Syria to run Freedom Hospital with Yasmin.

SALEM

An inpatient in Freedom Hospital, Salem suffers memory loss having survived a battle between the regular army and the rebels. No one knows his background. He seems to be around twenty-six or twenty-seven years old and his accent indicates he might come from a coastal town, maybe Latakia or Tartus.

WALID ABU QATADA

Born in 1972 in Homs. A former taxi driver, he stays out of the early peaceful demonstrations but joins the rebels when they take up arms. Seriously injured in combat, he has been an inpatient at the hospital for some time. He claims to be pro-Muslim Brotherhood, but his true beliefs are in fact closer to the Salafist jihadi.

ZAHABIAH

Born in 1992 in Ma'arrat al-Numan near Idlib, Zahabiah comes from a conservative Sunni family that refuses to allow her to study in the co-educational environment of a university. When the civil war breaks out she flees her hometown with her five brothers, who join the Free Syrian Army. To help Zahabiah's family, Yasmin hires her as the cook at Freedom Hospital. Zahabiah is Haval's girlfriend.

DR FAWAZ AL-FAWAZ

Born in 1979 in Latakia, Fawaz is from an Alawite family but is a self-professed agnostic. He meets Yasmin for the first time at a demonstration in Duma, near Damascus. He and Yasmin go on to provide medical assistance in several Syrian towns. When Yasmin announces that she's going to open an underground hospital, Fawaz decides to volunteer as one of the doctors.

THE COLONEL

Born in 1951 in the suburbs of Homs, the Colonel comes from a traditional Alawite family with close ties to the Assad family. He studied engineering in Russia and was high up in the Syrian communist party that ran against Hafez al-Assad in the late 1970s. He then left the party to join the army, where he has spent his career. He was one of the first officials to authorise the use of firearms against civilians at peaceful demonstrations.

Chapter 1

SPRING

MARCH 2012:
40,000 KILLED SINCE
THE REVOLUTION BEGAN.

YASMIN, WHERE THE HELL ARE THEY? THEY'RE OVER TWO HOURS LATE!

RELAX, SOPHIE. THEY'LL BE HERE SOON.

ABU TAYSIR, ABU AZAB, ALLOW ME TO INTRODUCE SOPHIE.

SHE SPEAKS PERFECT ARABIC.

MASHA'ALLAH, MASHA'ALLAH. I ADMIRE YOUR COURAGE, YOUNG LADY. WHERE ARE YOU FROM?

I'M SYRIAN. BOTH MY PARENTS ARE FROM HERE, BUT WE LIVE IN FRANCE.

WE LEFT A LONG TIME AGO.

OH, I HAVE A HEADACHE TOO, COULD I HAVE ONE, ABU AZAB?

OF COURSE, SOPHIE. HERE YOU GO.

16

THERE, THAT'S THE SIGNAL, IT'S SAFE TO GO.

ABU TAYSIR IS ONE OF THE LEADERS OF THE REBEL ARMY. YOU SHOULD TALK TO HIM, SOPHIE.

I'D LOVE TO.

IT WOULD BE MY PLEASURE, INSH'ALLAH.

I SHOULD MENTION I HAVE A SON, TAYSIR.*

HE'S A BRILLIANT BOY. SPEAKS FRENCH.

SOPHIE, YOU SEEM LIKE A CHARMING GIRL, WHAT DO YOU SAY?

ERM, WHAT DO YOU MEAN?

HAHAHA, ABU TAYSIR IS PROPOSING THAT YOU MARRY TAYSIR, SYRIAN STYLE...

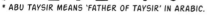

* ABU TAYSIR MEANS 'FATHER OF TAYSIR' IN ARABIC.

17

GOODBYE, MY DEARS, TAKE CARE OF YOURSELVES, MAY ALLAH PROTECT YOU.

WHY HAVE YOU STUCK A PHOTO OF THAT ANIMAL ON YOUR CAR?

LET'S GO, WE'VE GOT TO PICK SOMEONE UP ON THE WAY.

IT'S A FRONT, WE'RE ABOUT TO GO THROUGH A PRO-BASHAR DISTRICT.

ARE THAT WOMAN AND HER GIANT CAT COMING WITH US?

JUST THE CAT.

MEOW

GET GOING, IT'S LATE.

UNDERSTOOD. THANKS, OM FAISAL.

OOOH, HE'S SO CUTE.

HIS OWNER WAS KILLED YESTERDAY.

DO YOU HAVE A VETERINARY ARM AT THE HOSPITAL?

HAHA HAHA!

21

THERE WAS A SKIRMISH, HE WAS THE ONLY SURVIVOR.

MMM. AND WILL WE BE SLEEPING IN THE HOSPITAL?

YES.

WE'VE ALREADY PASSED THIS WAY, HAVEN'T WE?

DON'T WORRY, SOPHIE, I KNOW MY HOME TOWN, YOU'RE IN SAFE HANDS.

YASMIN, STOP THE CAR! DID YOU SEE THAT?

SEE WHAT, SOPHIE?

TWO MEN DRESSED LIKE SOMETHING FROM THE MIDDLE AGES.

YOU MUST HAVE IMAGINED IT. YOU'RE TIRED.

ALSO, YOU ALWAYS SAY YOU FEEL LIKE YOU'RE IN AN OLD FILM WHEN YOU COME TO SYRIA.

SO MUCH OLD-SCHOOL STUFF, THE VINTAGE CARS... YOU SAY IT EVERY TIME.

MIAOW

AAAAGHH

31

TAKE HIM INSIDE BEFORE HE ATTRACTS ATTENTION.

Y-YOU SEE, HAVAL? Y-Y-YOUR STUPID MASK S-S-SCARED HIM.

SORRY, ELIJAH! BUT I WON'T BE THE SORRY ONE WHEN IT SAVES ME FROM A CHEMICAL ATTACK.

O-OK, S-STOP TALKING AND H-HELP ME CARRY HIM.

ANYWAY, IT'S YOUR UGLY MUG THAT FREAKED HIM OUT.

BLAM

RIGHT FOOT FIRST.

THEN THE LEFT.

LADIES AND GENTLEMEN, LET'S BEGIN!

I LOVE HOSPITALS: DRUGS ON TAP.

LISTEN CAREFULLY, I WON'T SAY THIS TWICE.

OVER THERE, THROUGH THAT WINDOW YOU CAN SPY ON THE NEIGHBOURS.

BAAAA

LET ME INTRODUCE YOU TO OUR BEST FRIEND, AND OUR ONLY WINDOW ON THE WORLD. WE CALL HER SAMIRA.

HERE WE HAVE ABU QATADA, OR WALID, EX-TAXI DRIVER TURNED FERVENT SALAFIST: HE READS THE QURAN ALL DAY LONG. HE FOUGHT WITH THE REBELS.

OH AND I FORGOT TO INTRODUCE THE MOST IMPORTANT PERSON OF ALL...

ME! I'M HAVAL. PHILOSOPHER-IN-RESIDENCE

I WAS DOING MILITARY SERVICE WHEN THE REVOLUTION BROKE OUT.

I WAS ORDERED TO FIRE ON CIVILIANS DURING A MARCH. I REFUSED.

DROPPED MY GUN AND JOINED THE DEMONSTRATION.

MY DEAR FORMER COLLEAGUES PUMPED ME FULL OF BULLETS.

41

I DON'T KNOW. THE LAST THING I REMEMBER IS LOOKING DOWN THE BARREL OF A GUN.

BY THE WAY, SORRY FOR BEING ROUGH WITH YOU THE OTHER DAY.

BUT THIS IS AN UNDERGROUND HOSPITAL. WE HAD TO STOP YOU BEFORE SOMEONE SPOTTED YOU IN THE STREET.

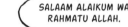

SALAAM ALAIKUM WA RAHMATU ALLAH.

SALAAM ALAIKUM WA RAHMATU ALLAH.

BROTHER SALEM, KEEP YOUR BEARD AND JOIN THE JIHAD, INSH'ALLAH.

I DON'T THINK HE'S ONE OF YOUR BROTHERS, WALID. HE WAS CLEAN-SHAVEN WHEN HE GOT HERE.

THANK YOU, DR YASMIN.

IT'S A COVER.

ACTUALLY, I'M NOT A DOCTOR, I'M A PHARMACIST. YOU CAN CALL ME YASMIN.

WHERE ARE WE EXACTLY?

THIS WAS MY GRANDFATHER'S HOUSE. HE LEFT IT TO MY FATHER AND HIS BROTHERS SO THEY COULD TURN IT INTO A HOSPITAL.

LOOKS MORE LIKE A RESTAURANT TO ME.

MY FATHER WORKED HARD TO SET THIS PLACE UP AS A HOSPITAL THIRTY YEARS AGO. HE JUST NEEDED MINISTERIAL APPROVAL.

BUT THE MINISTER AT THE TIME WAS CORRUPT AND GREEDY. HE MUST HAVE WATCHED 'THE GODFATHER' A FEW TOO MANY TIMES.

45

HE ASKED MY FATHER FOR A FIFTY PER CENT SHARE IN THE HOSPITAL IN EXCHANGE FOR THE PERMIT.

HE USED HIS CONNECTIONS TO THE PRESIDENT TO PUT PRESSURE ON MY FATHER.

SOME SAY THAT HE WAS THE ONE IN CHARGE OF LAUNDERING MONEY FOR THE PRESIDENT.

'THE GODFATHER'?

SORRY, IT'S A FILM. YOU WOULDN'T REMEMBER IT.

OH.

TO CUT A LONG STORY SHORT, THE REGIME WAS RUN BY A BUNCH OF MAFIOSI.

IN THE END, MY FATHER GOT AN OFFER FROM A GUY WHO WANTED TO RENT THE HOUSE AND RUN IT AS A RESTAURANT... WHICH WAS OPEN FOR THIRTY YEARS.

BUT WHEN THE REVOLUTION STARTED, THE RESTAURANT CLOSED.

WHEN I GOT OUT OF PRISON, I CAME BACK HERE TO FOLLOW MY FATHER'S DREAM.

AND TURN IT INTO A HOSPITAL, TREATING REBEL FIGHTERS FREE OF CHARGE.

IF YOU OPPOSE THE REGIME, YOU CAN'T GO NEAR THE PUBLIC HOSPITALS, THEY'RE SWARMING WITH INFORMERS AND SOLDIERS ON THE LOOKOUT.

YAZAN SAW IT WITH HIS OWN EYES: MEN, WOMEN AND CHILDREN TAKEN ON STRETCHERS INTO INTERROGATION CENTRES, NEVER TO COME OUT AGAIN.

DO YOU LOOK A BIT MORE LIKE YOURSELF?

I DON'T KNOW!

DRAGUNOV SNIPER RIFLE MADE IN RUSSIA, SYRIAN ARMY.

I HAVE IMPORTANT INFORMATION TO SHARE WITH EVERYONE.

THE ARMY HAS SET UP A NEW CHECKPOINT AT THE CITY GATES.

BE VERY CAREFUL IF IT'S ON YOUR PLANNED ROUTE OUT, OR IF YOU KNOW ANYONE ON THEIR WAY IN.

APOLOGIES FOR THE INTERRUPTION. KEEP IT UP.

WHAT THE - YOU TOLD ME YOU HAD NOTHING ON YOU!

TAKE THE BULLETS AND HIDE THEM IN A PACK OF CIGARETTES.

INSH'ALLAH, THEY WON'T FIND THEM.

ARE YOU **CRAZY**? WHAT IF THEY DO?

PUT THE PACK IN YOUR POCKET. THEY DON'T USUALLY BOTHER SEARCHING CLOTHES.

CHUCK THE **FUCKING** BULLETS OUT THE WINDOW!

IT'LL BE FINE.

KEEP YOUR COOL.

TTSSSSS

GOOD EVENING. TONIGHT, IN THE NEWS...

SYRIAN TV BROADCASTING PRO-ASSAD PROPAGANDA.

LOOK! OUR TOWN'S ON THE NEWS.

SHHHHH.

CLASHES IN THE NORTH OF THE COUNTRY TODAY.

OUR GLORIOUS ARMY KILLED THE TERRORIST MOHAMAD AL-SAMAN.

BASTARDS.

64

TALKING OF WHICH, TAYSIR, DO YOU KNOW ANY MORE ABOUT THOSE TWO MEN DRESSED IN MEDIEVAL ROBES, THE ONES SOPHIE SAW?

NO, I THINK SHE MUST HAVE IMAGINED IT.

AT THE TIME, I TOLD HER SHE WAS SEEING THINGS.

BUT I SAW THEM TOO. I DIDN'T WANT TO WORRY HER. DO YOU THINK THEY'RE AL-QAEDA?

SURELY NOT. PERHAPS THE REGIME SENT THEM TO SPREAD FEAR OF A FUNDAMENTALIST THREAT.

YOU KNOW THAT'S NONSENSE.

YOU SHOULD CHECK IT OUT. YOU KNOW AS WELL AS I DO THAT IT WOULD SUIT ASSAD IF ISLAMISTS TOOK CONTROL OF THE REVOLUTION.

SALEM, THAT'S THE PRISON WHERE YASMIN AND I WERE HELD.

WHY?

HAVE YOU REALLY FORGOTTEN EVERYTHING?

THE REVOLUTION BEGAN WHEN THEY STARTED TO SEE EVERYONE AS A POTENTIAL POLITICAL PRISONER. THEY EVEN STARTED LOCKING UP CHILDREN.

DO YOU REMEMBER WHEN THEY ARRESTED AND TORTURED SCHOOLBOYS AT DARAA?

THAT LADY WITH A PATCH SEEMS FAMILIAR.

IS THAT ELIJAH'S SISTER?

THAT'S MARIE COLVIN. AN AMERICAN JOURNALIST KILLED IN HOMS.

I MET HER THERE ONCE, MAY ALLAH BLESS HER.

* HABIBI MEANS 'BELOVED' IN ARABIC.

RELAX, HABIBI, WE'RE ALONE.

I'LL ASK YOUR FATHER FOR YOUR HAND ONE MORE TIME.

...

...

NOTHING HAS CHANGED SINCE THE LAST TIME, HAVAL.

FATHER WANTS ME TO MARRY A SAUDI WHO HAS DAUGHTERS OLDER THAN ME!

I WON'T GIVE IN TO HIM. LET'S GET MARRIED AND RUN AWAY.

I'M THE ONLY ONE WHO GETS TO DECIDE WHO I SPEND MY LIFE WITH.

WE'RE OPPRESSED BY THESE BACKWARD AND CONSERVATIVE VALUES.

HMMM.

YOUR BROTHER, ABU AZAB, IS FIGHTING FOR FREEDOM.

MMMM.

BUT IF HE KNEW ABOUT US, HE'D KILL US IN A HEARTBEAT.

IT'S BEEN TOO LONG.

WHERE HAVE YOU BEEN, MAN?

I WAS HELPING DOWN IN DAMASCUS.

WHERE'S YOUR CAR?

I DIDN'T REALLY NEED IT AND THE MONEY WILL KEEP THE HOSPITAL ON ITS FEET FOR ANOTHER MONTH OR TWO.

AND IN THE MEANTIME, THE DONKEY, JUHA OR THE KING WILL DIE.

IF YOU SAY SO. I THINK THE DONKEY ONLY HAS ANOTHER THREE MONTHS IN HIM, WE'RE SO CLOSE.

I BET THE REGIME WON'T LAST MORE THAN TWO. THE AMERICANS ARE OUT TO GET THEM.

SPEAKING OF AMERICANS, I HAVE TO LEAVE NEXT MONTH FOR MY DOCTORATE. BUT I CAN'T BEAR TO MISS ANYTHING HERE.

NO, YASMIN, YOU HAVE TO GO. WE WON'T STOP FIGHTING TILL ASSAD FALLS.

I KNOW.

DO YOU KNOW WHAT... YOUR FATHER AND GRANDFATHER WOULD BE PROUD OF YOU, FOLLOWING THEIR DREAM LIKE THIS.

FRAGMENTATION
MISSILE MADE IN
RUSSIA, SYRIAN ARMY.

MIAAAOWW

SHIT.

EVERYONE TO THE SHELTER!

LET ME TALK TO THAT IDIOT THERE.

LISTEN CAREFULLY, HERE'S THE DEAL, SON OF A BITCH.

SAY THAT BASHAR AL-ASSAD IS YOUR GOD AND YOU CAN GO FREE.

I SWEAR THAT AL-ASSAD IS MY ONLY GOD.

GOOD DOG, OFF YOU GO.

I SWEAR TO GOD, I'M GOING TO KILL THAT SON OF A BITCH ASSAD.

AL-ASSAD IS OUR ONLY GOD.

YOU SAID IT.

* QURAN AL-ANFAL SURAH 8, VERSE 17.

DSHK MADE IN RUSSIA, ABU TAYSIR MILITIA.

DSHK MADE IN RUSSIA, ABU TAYSIR MILITIA.

HAVE MERCY, LET ME GO. I'M INNOCENT.

ABU AZAB, MY SON.

WHEN WE'RE FIGHTING MONSTERS, WE MUST TAKE CARE NOT TO BECOME MONSTERS OURSELVES.

WE HAD NO CHOICE BUT TO TAKE UP ARMS TO PROTECT CIVILIANS. BASHAR WAS MASSACRING US IN OUR TENS OF THOUSANDS...

BUT WE'RE NOT FIGHTING TO REPLACE ONE DICTATOR WITH ANOTHER.

Chapter 2

SUMMER

I HOPE I'M PROVED WRONG, BUT I DON'T THINK THEY'RE GOING TO INTERVENE.

THANKS.

EURRK

103

*JAMAL MEANS 'BEAUTY' IN ARABIC.

S-S-SALEM, HAVE YOU GOT YOUR MEMORY BACK?

I DON'T KNOW WHY THAT CAME BACK TO ME.

I-I WAS F-F-FORCED TO TALK ON STATE T-TV TO SAY I'D BEEN INJURED IN A T-TERRORIST ATTACK.

I WAS F-FORCED TO LIE.

THE T-TRUTH IS, I W-WAS LOCKED UP BECAUSE OF WHAT I-I-I DID IN MY OLD HOME TOWN.

ONE D-DAY, I HEARD SHOOTING OUTSIDE THE JAIL. THE R-REBELS WERE TRYING TO G-G-GET US OUT.

THE G-G-GUARDS MADE US PAY FOR THAT ATTACK.

THEY DRAGGED ME OUT OF MY C-CELL AND BEAT ME WITH THEIR GUNS.

THE FIRST BLOW T-TOOK OUT MY EYE.

106

INSH'ALLAH, WE WILL AVENGE THEM.

I SWEAR TO ALLAH, ONCE I RECOVER, I'M GOING BACK TO FIGHT AND I WILL KILL EVERY ALAWITE I COME ACROSS.

WE SHOULD KILL EVERY LAST ALAWITE.

111

PAMM

BOMMMM

SHIT, I REALLY CAN'T SCORE TO SAVE MY LIFE.

PAMM

PAM

I HAD NO CHOICE.

THAT'S NOT WHY I WAS AVOIDING YOU.

THEN WHY? I THOUGHT YOU'D GONE OFF ME.

I WAS AFRAID YOU WERE OLD-SCHOOL AND THAT YOU'D ASK ME TO MARRY YOU OR SOMETHING. WELL, YOU KNOW, THE USUAL STORY...

WHAT GAVE YOU THAT IDEA?

I DON'T KNOW... PLENTY OF MEN ARE COOL AT FIRST, THEN THEY START TO CHANGE WHEN THINGS GET SERIOUS...

I FELL IN LOVE THE DAY WE MET AT THE DEMONSTRATION.

BUT I WANTED OUR STORY TO BEGIN AFTER THE REVOLUTION.

SUKHOI SU-24 MADE IN RUSSIA, SYRIAN ARMY.

MISSILES ARE ARMED.

FIRE.

ARE YOU SURE THERE ARE NO CIVILIANS IN THE AREA?

FIRE THE MISSILES, FOOL. THAT'S AN ORDER.

YES, SIR

AAAGH, MUMMY, HELP ME, AAAGH!

IT'S OUR ONLY HOPE. IF WE CAN TAKE THE AIRPORT, WE CAN GET MORE WEAPONS TO FIGHT, AND EVEN SOME ANTI-BALLISTIC MISSILES.

THEY WOULDN'T BE ABLE TO ATTACK US. WE WOULD CONTROL THE AIRSPACE.

YOU KNOW VERY WELL THAT I ONLY WANT TO PROTECT CIVILIANS.

WHEN ARE YOU PLANNING THE ATTACK?

SOON. IN THE NEXT TWO OR THREE DAYS.

AND WHY ARE YOU WARNING US?

I'VE TOLD YOU, I NEED YOUR HELP.

TAKE THIS WALKIE-TALKIE. WE CAN STAY IN CONTACT.

GO ON, TAKE IT. WE NEED YOU ON THE FRONT LINE.

KEEP DREAMING.

DSHK MADE IN RUSSIA, ABU TAYSIR MILITIA.

CHOP CHOP

CHOP

VRRRMM

VrRrRR

MI-28 MADE IN RUSSIA, SYRIAN ARMY.

CHOP CHOP CHOP

TRANSLATION: 'THERE IS A SNIPER OPPOSITE.'

HELLO. COLONEL? CAN YOU HEAR ME?

IT'S ABU TAYSIR, OF THE FREE SYRIAN ARMY.

INSH'ALLAH, YOU ARE SURROUNDED BY 2,000 REBELS.

AND THEY'RE PREPARED TO FIGHT, TO THE DEATH IF NECESSARY.

COLONEL!

I'LL GIVE YOU TEN MINUTES TO REFLECT ON THAT.

WE'RE ALL SYRIANS. LET'S NOT SHED ANY MORE BLOOD TODAY.

GO FUCK YOURSELF, ABU TAYSIR.

THE SYRIAN ARMY, OUR OWN FLESH AND BLOOD, PAID FOR BY OUR TAXES, HAS BECOME OUR ENEMY.

MY HEART BREAKS EVERY TIME WE KILL AN ARMY SOLDIER. THEY ARE OUR BROTHERS AND OUR SONS.

OR WHEN WE DESTROY A BUILDING OR A RESERVOIR PAID FOR BY THE SYRIAN PEOPLE.

WE MUST STOP FUNDING AN ARMY THAT KILLS ITS OWN PEOPLE AND PROTECTS A DICTATOR.

THE COLONEL AND I ARE THE SAME AGE.

EVEN IF WE COME FROM DIFFERENT BACKGROUNDS, OUR PATHS HAVE ALREADY CROSSED.

SUBHAN ALLAH, MAY GOD WATCH OVER SYRIA.

THE COLONEL KNOWS ME WELL, AND HE KNOWS I'M NOT JOKING.

I KNOW HE HAS ALREADY ISSUED THE ALERT.

HE IS PREPARING FOR COMBAT.

HE KNEW THAT I WAS LYING WHEN I SAID WE HAD 2,000 REBELS SURROUNDING HIS CAMP.

HE KNOWS WE'RE ONLY 1,451.

WHAT HE DOESN'T REALISE IS THAT 549 OF HIS OWN MEN ARE AGAINST THE REGIME.

THOSE MEN WERE FORCED TO ENROL AND THEIR FAMILIES WERE MISTREATED.

THEY ARE FULL OF RAGE AND HUNGRY FOR REVENGE.

144

AFTER MY APPEAL, BY NOW THEY SHOULD BE ARMED AND READY TO CLEAR THE CAMP FROM THE INSIDE.

 FIVE.

 FOUR.

 THREE.

 TWO.

 AND ONE.

GODDAMMIT!

BA AM

147

CHOP

CHOP

CHOP

CHOP

CHOP

149

154

155

156

157

سوريا : النظام يقصف مشفى الحرية بالبراميل المتفجرة

 427

3561

+ Add to   Share ••• More

👍 108 👎 2

Published 16 March, 2013

Catalogue   People of blogs
License   License Youtube standard

All Comments (4)

 Add a Comments

DRAGUNOV SNIPER RIFLE MADE IN RUSSIA, SYRIAN ARMY.

166

TSHSHSH

MORE THAN 6,000 PEOPLE HAVE LOST A LEG IN THIS WAR. AND THE 100,000 PEOPLE KILLED SINCE THE REVOLUTION BEGAN MAKE FOR ANOTHER 200,000 LEGS.

CrAACk

cRsSsh

SPLASH

OUR MARTYRS ARE HAPPY AND SMILING NOW. THEY ARE THE CHOSEN.

THE ANGELS OF DEATH HAVE ASKED THEM: 'WHO IS YOUR GOD?'

AND THEY HAVE ANSWERED: 'ALLAH IS OUR GOD AND MUHAMMAD IS HIS PROPHET.'

THEY HAVE ASKED: 'HOW WERE YOU KILLED?' 'FIGHTING FOR ALLAH.'

THE ANGELS HAVE PRONOUNCED: 'YOU ACTED WELL.' SO DRY YOUR TEARS. THE MARTYRS ARE NOT DEAD, THEY LIVE ON IN PARADISE, INSH'ALLAH.

Chapter 3

AUTUMN

IN THE RUINS OF THE HOSPITAL. A FEW WEEKS LATER: ANOTHER 2,386 KILLED.

SORRY, BOYS, I'VE GOT TO GET BACK TO WORK.

HOW ABOUT YOU, SALEM? HOW LONG HAVE YOU BEEN HERE?

AROUND SEVEN MONTHS. I'M PERFECTLY WELL.

WHO SHOT YOU?

I CAN'T REMEMBER.

IN FACT, I STOPPED BEING A PATIENT HERE TWO WEEKS AGO, BUT DR YAZAN - MAY HE REST IN PEACE - ASKED ME TO STAY AS I HAD NOWHERE TO GO.

YOU DON'T KNOW YOUR LUCK, SALEM.

WHAT DO YOU MEAN?

OH, OH NO.

YOU AND YOUR OCD, MAN. ROLL YOUR OWN JOINT IF YOU PREFER.

I DON'T KNOW HOW.

OK, LET ME.

I THINK I'VE FOUND A WAY FOR YOU TO GET TO SWITZERLAND.

I KNOW YOU'D PREFER GERMANY BUT YOU COULD LIVE IN THE GERMAN-SPEAKING BIT.

195

TO BRING ABOUT THE DREAM OF OUR GREAT MARTYR, SHEIKH OSAMA.

IN THE TIME OF THE CALIPHATE, MUSLIM RULE STRETCHED FROM INDIA TO SPAIN.

AND THE PROPHET MUHAMMAD PROMISED THAT DAMASCUS WOULD BE OUR CAPITAL ONCE AGAIN.

I HAVE GATHERED YOU ALL HERE TO ANNOUNCE THAT SOON WE WILL CELEBRATE THE GREAT ISLAMIC STATE OF IRAQ AND THE LEVANT.

AND THAT YOU SHOULD JOIN OUR FIGHT.

WHO IS READY TO PLEDGE ALLEGIANCE TO ABU BAKR AL-BAGHDADI, THE LEADER OF THE ISLAMIC STATE OF IRAQ AND THE LEVANT, AND TO ME, WALID ABU QATADA, YOUR PRINCE?

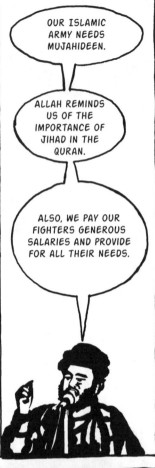

OUR ISLAMIC ARMY NEEDS MUJAHIDEEN.

ALLAH REMINDS US OF THE IMPORTANCE OF JIHAD IN THE QURAN.

ALSO, WE PAY OUR FIGHTERS GENEROUS SALARIES AND PROVIDE FOR ALL THEIR NEEDS.

THOSE WHO WISH TO JOIN US SHOULD TALK TO BROTHER AL-SAMERAI.

SALAAM ALAIKUM WA RAHMATULLAHI WA BARAKATUH.

THIS COULD BE MY WAY OUT.

IF I JOIN, I CAN SAVE THE MONEY TO ESCAPE.

SALAAM ALAIKUM WA RAHMATULLAHI WA BARAKATUH.

OK, PERFECT.

ALMOST THERE, A LITTLE TO THE RIGHT.

IS IT PLUGGED IN?

I STILL DON'T UNDERSTAND WHY THE NAME BOTHERS YOU.

IT'S NOT THE NAME, I JUST FIND THE SITUATION FUNNY, THIS SENSE OF DÉJÀ VU.

I FEEL LIKE I'VE GONE BACK IN TIME BY FOUR MONTHS.

NO, WE'RE STILL GOING FORWARD, EVEN IF THEY DEMOLISH THE HOSPITAL A HUNDRED TIMES...

Chapter 4

WINTER

213

AK-47 MADE
IN RUSSIA, ISLAMIC
STATE.

≡ YouTube

 الدولة الإسلامية 🔍

▶ ▶▶ ◀◀ ⏸ 🔊 207 / 215

سوريا: تدريبات الدولة الإسلامية العسكرية

 Tv ISIS ▶ OBSERVE **532**

➕ Add to ▶ share ⋯ Plus

Published 3 April 2013
Catalogue   loople of blogs
Liaison   License YouTube plus

All comments 151

 🖊 Add a comment

▼ ·

WHEN THE CHAHIBAS STEPPED IN, KILLING AND ARRESTING THOUSANDS OF PEOPLE.

THE STATE MACHINERY SPEWED OUT ITS PROPAGANDA.

SUDDENLY WE BECAME ARMED TERRORISTS OUT TO TERRIFY THE POPULATION.

MUSLIMS ARE NOT TERRORISTS. 'ISLAM' COMES FROM THE WORD 'PEACE'.

OUR STORY REMINDS ME OF THE FABLE OF THE GOAT AND THE WOLF, WALLA.

'THE MOTHER GOAT STOOD BY WHEN THE WOLF ATE HER FIRST KID, AND HER SECOND...

... BUT WHEN HE WENT FOR THE THIRD, SHE ATTACKED HIM, AND THE ANIMALS WHO WITNESSED THE SCENE SAID THAT THE GOAT HAD BULLIED THE POOR WOLF.'

THE WEST SEES US AS TERRORISTS, BECAUSE THEY ARE AFRAID OF THE TRUE TEACHINGS OF ISLAM.

THE MUSLIM EMPIRE IS THE GREATEST THING EVER TO HAPPEN TO HUMANITY.

WE LOST OURSELVES WHEN WE BETRAYED ISLAM'S TRUE TEACHINGS.

NO ONE WILL SAY IT, BUT THE REGIME IS PROPPED UP BY INFIDELS...

HELLO, ABU TAYSIR, CAN YOU STILL HEAR ME?

LOUD AND CLEAR.

YASMIN WILL THINK YOU'RE JUST AS BAD IF YOU DON'T DO SOMETHING.

AS BAD AS WHO, DEAR FAWAZ AL-FAWAZ? WHAT ARE YOU TALKING ABOUT?

YASMIN THINKS YOU'RE NOT REALLY FIGHTING AGAINST ABU QATADA AND HIS LOT.

I DON'T REALLY SEE WHAT MORE I CAN DO. I'M FIGHTING AGAINST THE REGIME, IRAN, HEZBOLLAH AND ALL THEIR ALLIES.

SO FAR, I HAVE LOST MORE THAN A HUNDRED OF MY BEST MEN.

EIGHT WERE KILLED BY ABU QATADA. I'M DOING ALL I CAN.

I KNOW YOU ARE, ABU TAYSIR. I REALLY DO.

LISTEN, ABU TAYSIR, I UNDERSTAND.

BUT JUST BECAUSE YOU'RE FIGHTING DIFFERENT ENEMIES ON SEVERAL FRONTS...

...DOESN'T MEAN YOU HAVE THE RIGHT TO LOSE CONTROL.

I KNOW IT'S UNINTENDED, BUT YOU'RE STARTING TO ACT LIKE A WAR LORD.

AND TO MAKE MATTERS WORSE, YOUR MEN ARE DEFECTING TO ABU QATADA.

YASMIN WON'T FORGIVE YOU IF YOU DO NOTHING.

I UNDERSTAND, BUT YOU'RE NOT BEING FAIR. I ADMIT I'VE MADE MISTAKES.

THEIR MOVEMENT IS QUICKLY TAKING HOLD OF ENTIRE TOWNS. I'M IN TOUCH WITH THE REBELS AND WE WILL HANDLE IT.

I'M COMING UP TO A CHECKPOINT. SOMETHING'S NOT RIGHT. I'LL CALL YOU BACK.

MAYBE WE SHOULD PLEDGE ALLEGIANCE AFTER ALL, AT LEAST WE'D GET SOME DECENT FOOD!

ANYWAY... LET'S CHANGE THE SUBJECT, TODAY'S A DAY FOR CELEBRATING.

SOPHIE HAS FINALLY FINISHED HER FILM AND SOON THE WORLD WILL SEE WHAT'S REALLY BEEN GOING ON HERE.

AND HAVAL AND ZAHABIAH'S VISAS HAVE COME THROUGH, THEY'RE LEAVING US.

I HOPE YOU'LL BE HAPPY IN SWITZERLAND, EVEN THOUGH YOU'VE ALWAYS DREAMT OF GERMANY.

IT'S MORE THAN A DREAM, I LOVE GERMANY. I CAN'T HELP IT, ALL KURDS LOVE GERMANY.

WE HAVE A JOKE ABOUT IT.

ALLAHU AKBAR

THANK YOU FOR COMING TONIGHT, IT'S WONDERFUL TO SEE SO MANY OF YOU.

I APOLOGISE BUT I CAN'T SAY MUCH TONIGHT.

I HAVE TO GO. EXCUSE ME.

THIS COULD BE USEFUL.

HELLO, KITTY.

I CAN CONQUER MY OBSESSIONS.

I CAN DO IT.

I CAN TOUCH THIS DOOR HANDLE WITH MY BARE HANDS.

AND OPEN THIS DAMN DOOR.

I PROMISED YASMIN I'D GET OVER MY MANIAS. I WILL DO IT.

CLACK

265

YOU KNOW, YASMIN, THERE WAS SOME TRUTH IN MY MEMORY PROBLEMS. I REALLY DON'T KNOW WHO SHOT ME.

I REMEMBER A GUY HOLDING A GUN, BUT I HAVE NO IDEA WHERE OR WHO IT WAS.

WHY ARE YOU HELPING US?

IN HALF AN HOUR WE'LL BE AT THE BORDER.

I'LL LEAVE YOU THERE.

BUT YOU HAVEN'T TOLD ME WHY YOU'RE DOING THIS FOR US. IS IT OUT OF GRATITUDE, OR DID YOU REALISE YOUR MISTAKE?

OK.

BEFORE COMING HERE, I WORKED FOR THE MUKHABARAT*.

NOTHING SPECIAL. I HAD TO INFILTRATE THE OPPOSITION AND SPY ON THEM.

* SYRIAN INTELLIGENCE AGENCY.

268

275

Chapter 5

SPRING, AGAIN

REFUGEE CAMP, SYRIAN–TURKISH BORDER.
THREE MONTHS LATER: ANOTHER 12,569 PEOPLE KILLED.

THE SPRING GOES ON...

POSTSCRIPT

When I fled Syria, on 17 August 2011, my first destination was Egypt. A few months in, I was in a taxi and the driver started asking me questions about Syria. He didn't understand the first thing about what was happening, and he even asked me if Bashar al-Assad was on the side of the Free Syrian Army... I realised that the absence of a free press in Syria had led to a massive lack of understanding, and while official Syrian media outfits were transmitting nothing but pro-Assad propaganda, pro-rebel media were no less guilty of churning out propaganda of their own. When I arrived in France in 2012, I saw that people's confusion about the situation in Syria was even greater.

I don't think anyone can capture exactly what is happening in Syria, even those on the ground right now. I decided to write *Freedom Hospital* to reflect the situation as I see it, not to explain it. I haven't tried to be neutral, and I can't claim to be depicting an exact reality, but I needed to give voice to everything that had been stuck in my throat since the beginning of the revolution.

I began this project in 2012 and it has taken nearly four years to complete. I chose to blend fiction and fact to avoid having to explain what was true or false. I'm interested in showing how events unfolded in a personal way. To tell Yasmin's story, and the stories of the other protagonists, I drew on real events that I witnessed with my own eyes before leaving Syria, and on the lived experiences of people I know. Some of my friends and acquaintances have stayed in Syria, others have since left, like me, and are now living in exile, in Europe or the United States.

For the purposes of the book, I invented a small rural town, Houria, which is an amalgam of many towns in the north of Syria, with a mosque presiding over the central square. It is on this square that Yasmin set up her clandestine hospital. The layout of the roads and buildings that I've drawn can be found in most towns and villages in Syria. Finally, I integrated images and text taken directly from the news into the story. For instance, the sequence on pages 154–5 is taken from a YouTube video streamed after a bombardment. I also used photos taken during demonstrations, extracts from speeches, and the propaganda slogans used by different factions in the course of the conflict.

Hamid Sulaiman
February 2016

ACKNOWLEDGEMENTS

This book has been selected to receive financial assistance from English PEN's Writers in Translation programme supported by Bloomberg and Arts Council England. English PEN exists to promote literature and its understanding, uphold writers' freedoms around the world, campaign against the persecution and imprisonment of writers for stating their views, and promote the friendly co-operation of writers and free exchange of ideas.

Each year, a dedicated committee of professionals selects books that are translated into English from a wide variety of foreign languages. We award grants to UK publishers to help translate, promote, market and champion these titles. Our aim is to celebrate books of outstanding literary quality, which have a clear link to the PEN charter and promote free speech and intercultural understanding.

In 2011, Writers in Translation's outstanding work and contribution to diversity in the UK literary scene was recognised by Arts Council England. English PEN was awarded a threefold increase in funding to develop its support for world writing in translation.

www.englishpen.org